In
1935 if you wanted to
read a good book, you needed
either a lot of money or a library card.
Cheap paperbacks were available, but their
poor production generally mirrored the quality
between the covers. One weekend that year,
Allen Lane, Managing Director of The Bodley Head,
having spent the weekend visiting Agatha Christie,
found himself on a platform at Exeter station trying to
find something to read for his journey back to London.
He was appalled by the quality of the material he had to
choose from. Everything that Allen Lane achieved from that
day until his death in 1970 was based on a passionate belief
in the existence of 'a vast reading public for *intelligent*
books at a low price'. The result of his momentous vision
was the birth not only of Penguin, but of the 'paperback
revolution'. Quality writing became available for the price of
a packet of cigarettes, literature became a mass medium
for the first time, a nation of book-borrowers became a
nation of book-buyers – and the very concept of book
publishing was changed for ever. Those founding
principles – of quality and value, with an overarching
belief in the fundamental importance of reading –
have guided everything the company has
done since 1935. Sir Allen Lane's
pioneering spirit is still very much alive
at Penguin in 2005. Here's to
the next 70 years!

MORE THAN A BUSINESS

'We decided it was time to end the almost customary half-hearted manner in which cheap editions were produced – as though the only people who could possibly want cheap editions must belong to a lower order of intelligence. We, however, believed in the existence in this country of a vast reading public for intelligent books at a low price, and staked everything on it'
Sir Allen Lane, 1902–1970

'The Penguin Books are splendid value for sixpence, so splendid that if other publishers had any sense they would combine against them and suppress them'
George Orwell

'More than a business … a national cultural asset'
Guardian

'When you look at the whole Penguin achievement you know that it constitutes, in action, one of the more democratic successes of our recent social history'
Richard Hoggart

Doctrines and Visions

NOAM CHOMSKY

PENGUIN BOOKS

PENGUIN BOOKS

Published by the Penguin Group
Penguin Books Ltd, 80 Strand, London WC2R ORL, England
Penguin Group (USA) Inc., 375 Hudson Street, New York, New York 10014, USA
Penguin Group (Canada), 10 Alcorn Avenue, Toronto, Ontario, Canada M4V 3B2
(a division of Pearson Penguin Canada Inc.)
Penguin Ireland, 25 St Stephen's Green, Dublin 2, Ireland
(a division of Penguin Books Ltd)
Penguin Group (Australia), 250 Camberwell Road, Camberwell, Victoria 3124,
Australia (a division of Pearson Australia Group Pty Ltd)
Penguin Books India Pvt Ltd, 11 Community Centre,
Panchsheel Park, New Delhi – 110 017, India
Penguin Group (NZ), cnr Airborne and Rosedale Roads, Albany,
Auckland 1310, New Zealand (a division of Pearson New Zealand Ltd)
Penguin Books (South Africa) (Pty) Ltd, 24 Sturdee Avenue,
Rosebank 2196, South Africa

Penguin Books Ltd, Registered Offices: 80 Strand, London WC2R ORL, England

www.penguin.com

Hegemony or Survival first published in the USA by Metropolitan Books 2003
First published in Great Britain by Hamish Hamilton 2004
This extract published as a Pocket Penguin 2005

1

Copyright © Aviva Chomsky, Diane Chomsky and Harry Chomsky, 2003
All rights reserved

The moral right of the author has been asserted

Set in 10.5/12.5pt Monotype Dante
Typeset by Palimpsest Book Production Limited
Polmont, Stirlingshire
Printed in England by Clays Ltd, St Ives plc

Contents

Priorities and Prospects

A few years ago, one of the great figures of contemporary biology, Ernst Mayr, published some reflections on the likelihood for success in the search for extraterrestrial intelligence (SETI).[1]* Mayr took exception to the conclusions of astrophysicists who confidently expected to find higher intelligence throughout the universe. He considered the prospects of success very low. His reasoning had to do with the adaptive value of what we call 'higher intelligence', meaning the particular human form of intellectual organization. Mayr estimated the number of species since the origin of life at about 50 billion, only one of which 'achieved the kind of intelligence needed to establish a civilization'. It did so very recently, perhaps a hundred thousand years ago. It is generally assumed that only one small breeding group survived, of which we are all descendants, apparently with very little genetic variation. What we call 'civilizations' developed near the end of this brief moment of evolutionary time, and are 'inevitably short-lived'.

Mayr speculates that higher intelligence may not be favored by selection. The history of life on Earth, he concluded, refutes the claim that 'it is better to be smart than to be stupid', at least judging by biological success: beetles and bacteria, for example, are far more successful

* The notes for this work can be found at www.happybirthday penguin.com

than primates in these terms, and that is generally true of creatures that fill a specific niche or can undergo rapid genetic change. He also made the rather somber observation that 'the average life expectancy of a species is about 100,000 years'.

We are entering a period of human life that may provide an answer to the question of whether it is better to be smart than stupid – whether there is intelligent life on Earth, in some sense of 'intelligence' that might be admired by a sensible extraterrestrial observer, could one exist. The most hopeful prospect is that the question will not be answered: if it receives a definite answer, that answer can only be that humans were a kind of 'biological error', using their allotted 100,000 years to destroy themselves and, in the process, much else. The species has surely developed the capacity to do just that, and our hypothetical extraterrestrial observer might conclude that they have demonstrated that capacity throughout their history, dramatically in the past few hundred years, with an assault on the environment that sustains life, on the diversity of more complex organisms, and with cold and calculated savagery, on each other as well.

Two Superpowers

The year 2003 opened with many indications that concerns about human survival are all too realistic. To mention just a few examples, in October 2002 it was learned that a possibly terminal nuclear war was barely avoided, by a near miracle, forty years earlier. Immediately after this startling discovery, the Bush administration unilaterally blocked UN efforts to ban the militarization of space, a serious threat to survival. It also terminated international negotiations to prevent biological warfare, and moved to ensure that it would have no choice but to attack Iraq despite popular opposition at home and abroad that was entirely without historical precedent.

Aid organizations with extensive experience in Iraq, and studies by respected medical organizations, warned that the planned invasion might precipitate a humanitarian catastrophe. The warnings were ignored by Washington and evoked little media interest. A high-level US task force concluded that attacks with weapons of mass destruction (WMD) within the United States are 'likely', and would become more so in the event of war with Iraq. Many specialists and intelligence and security agencies, in the US and elsewhere, agreed. Such concerns were heightened by the release in September 2002 of the Bush administration's National Security Strategy, which declared the right to resort to force to eliminate any perceived challenge to US global hegemony, now or ever. Specialists and intelligence agencies warned again that Washington's belligerence was increasing the long-term threat of international terrorism and proliferation of WMD. These warnings too were dismissed, indicating how human lives, including American lives, rank in the scale of priorities.

In the same month, September 2002, a propaganda campaign was launched to depict Saddam Hussein as an imminent threat to the United States and to insinuate that he was responsible for the 9-11 atrocities and was planning others. The campaign, timed to the onset of the mid-term congressional elections, was highly successful in shifting attitudes. It soon drove American public opinion off the global spectrum, enabling the administration to achieve electoral aims and to establish Iraq as a proper 'test case' for the newly announced doctrine of resort to force at will.

The administration then proceeded to antagonize even its closest allies by blocking efforts in the World Trade Organization to provide inexpensive drugs to people dying from treatable diseases, indicating once again that huge profits for (heavily subsidized) US pharmaceutical corporations are a much higher priority than the tens of millions of lives that could easily be saved.[2]

President Bush and associates also persisted in undermining international efforts to reduce threats to the environment that are recognized to be severe, with pretexts that barely concealed their devotion to narrow sectors of private power. The administration's Climate Change Science Program (CCSP), wrote *Science Magazine* editor Donald Kennedy, is a travesty that 'included no recommendations for emission limitation or other forms of mitigation', contenting itself with 'voluntary reduction targets, which, even if met, would allow US emission rates to continue to grow at around 14% per decade'. The CCSP did not even consider the likelihood, suggested by 'a growing body of evidence', that the short-term warming changes it ignores 'will trigger an abrupt nonlinear process', producing dramatic temperature changes that could carry extreme risks for the United States, Europe, and other temperate zones, as well as others. The Bush administration's 'contemptuous pass on multilateral engagement with the global warming problem', Kennedy continued, is the 'stance that began the long continuing process of eroding its friendships in Europe', leading to 'smoldering resentment'.[3]

By October 2002, it was becoming hard to miss the fact that the world is 'more concerned about the unbridled use of American power than it is about the threat posed by Saddam Hussein', and 'is as intent on limiting the giant's power as it is in taking away the despot's weapons'.[4] World concerns mounted in the months that followed as the giant made clear its intent to attack Iraq even if the UN inspections it reluctantly tolerated failed to unearth weapons that would provide a pretext. By December, support for Washington's war plans scarcely reached 10 percent almost anywhere, according to international polls. Two months later, after enormous worldwide protests, the press reported that 'there may still be two superpowers on the planet: the United States and world public opinion' ('the United States' here meaning state power, not the public, not even elite opinion).[5]

By early 2003, fear of the United States had reached remarkable heights throughout the world, along with distrust of and often loathing for the political leadership.[6] If they continue on their present course they may create much broader antagonism to the country they are turning into a pariah nation, regarded by many as the greatest threat to peace – which may, today, translate as survival.

A neutral observer might be puzzled by what appear to be calculated and deliberate efforts to engender resentment, fear, and hatred. A rational conclusion would be that such consequences matter no more to Washington planners than tens of millions of deaths, immeasurable agony and suffering, or even prospects for decent survival, when ranked against the imperatives of power and profit.

Dismissal of elementary human rights and needs was matched by a display of contempt for democracy for which no parallel comes easily to mind, accompanied by professions of sincere dedication to human rights and democracy. If this were happening in Andorra it would be merely comical. Perhaps what is really happening might amuse some hypothetical extraterrestrial observer. It does not, however, amuse the second superpower. For good reason. What is unfolding should be deeply disturbing to those on Earth who have some concerns about the world they are leaving to their grandchildren.

Though Bush planners are at an extreme end of the traditional US policy spectrum, their programs and doctrines have many precursors, in US history and among earlier aspirants to global dominance, even among those with lesser ambitions. More ominously, the decisions may not be irrational within a framework deeply rooted in prevailing ideology and the institutions within which it takes shape. There is ample historical precedent for the willingness of leaders to threaten or resort to violence in the face of significant risk of catastrophe. The stakes are far higher today. The choice between hegemony and survival has rarely, if ever, been so starkly posed.

Let us try to unravel some of the many strands that enter into this complex tapestry, focusing attention on the world power that proclaims global hegemony. Its actions and their guiding doctrines must be a primary concern for everyone on the planet, particularly so, of course, for Americans. Many enjoy unusual advantages and freedom, hence the ability to shape the future, and should face with

care and integrity the responsibilities that are the immediate corollary of such privilege.

Enemy Territory

Those who want to face their responsibilities with a genuine
commitment to democracy and freedom – even to decent
survival – should recognize, without illusion, the barriers
that stand in the way. In violent and terrorist states, these
are not concealed. In more democratic societies, barriers
are more subtle. While methods differ sharply from more
brutal to more free societies, the goals are in many ways
similar: to ensure that the 'great beast', as Alexander
Hamilton called the people, does not stray from its proper
confines.

The Enemy at Home

Controlling the general population has always been a domi-
nant concern of power and privilege, particularly since the
first modern democratic revolution in seventeenth-century
England. The self-described 'men of best quality' were
appalled as a 'giddy multitude of beasts in men's shapes'
rejected the basic framework of the civil conflict raging in
England between king and parliament. They rejected rule
by king *or* parliament and called for government 'by
countrymen like ourselves, that know our wants', not
by 'knights and gentlemen that make us laws, that are
chosen for fear and do but oppress us, and do not know
the people's sores'. The men of best quality recognized

7

that if the people are so 'depraved and corrupt' as to 'confer places of power and trust upon wicked and undeserving men, they forfeit their power in this behalf unto those that are good, though but a few'. Almost three centuries later, Wilsonian idealism – as it is standardly termed – adopted a rather similar stance. Abroad, it is Washington's responsibility to ensure that government is in the hands of 'the good, though but a few'. At home, it is necessary to safeguard a system of elite decision-making and public ratification ('polyarchy' in the terminology of political science).[7]

As president, Woodrow Wilson himself did not shrink from severely repressive policies even within the United States, but such measures are not normally available where popular struggles have won a substantial measure of freedom and rights. By Wilson's day, it was widely recognized by elite sectors in the US and Britain that, within their societies, coercion was a tool of diminishing utility, and that it would be necessary to devise new means to tame the beast, primarily through control of opinion and attitude. Huge industries have since developed devoted to these ends.[8]

Wilson's own view was that an elite of gentlemen with 'elevated ideals' must be empowered to preserve 'stability and righteousness';[9] 'stability' is a code word for subordination to existing power systems, and righteousness will be determined by the rulers. Leading public intellectuals agreed. 'The public must be put in its place,' Walter Lippmann declared in his progressive essays on democracy. That goal could be achieved in part through 'the manufacture of consent', 'a self-conscious art and regular organ of popular government'. This 'revolution [in the] practice of democracy' should enable a 'specialized class [of] responsible men' to manage the 'common interests [that] very largely elude public opinion entirely'. In essence, the Leninist ideal. Lippmann had observed the revolution in the practice of democracy first-hand, as a member of Wilson's Committee on Public Information, which was established to coordinate wartime propaganda and achieved great success in whipping the population into war fever.

The 'responsible men' who are the proper decision-makers, Lippmann continued, 'have obtained their training . . . in the law schools and law offices and in business', and in their 'executive action' they must 'live free of the trampling and the roar of a bewildered herd . . . ignorant and meddlesome outsiders', who are to be 'spectators', not 'participants'. The herd do have a 'function': to trample periodically in support of one or another element of the natural leadership class in an election, then to return to private pursuits. Unstated is that the responsible men gain that status not by virtue of any special talent or knowledge, but by subordination to the systems of actual power and loyalty to their operative principles. Basic decisions over social and economic life are to be kept within institutions with top-down authoritarian control, while within a diminished public arena, the participation of the beast is to be limited.

Just how narrow the public arena should be is a matter of debate. Neoliberal initiatives of the past thirty years have been designed to restrict it, leaving basic decision-making within largely unaccountable private tyrannies, linked closely to one another and to a few powerful states. Democracy can then survive, but in sharply reduced form. Reagan–Bush sectors have taken an extreme position in this regard, but the policy spectrum is fairly narrow. Some

9

argue that it scarcely exists at all, mocking the pundits who 'actually make a living contrasting the finer points of the sitcoms on NBC with those broadcast on CBS' during election campaigns: 'Through tacit agreement the two major parties approach the contest for the presidency [as] political kabuki [in which] the players know their roles and everyone sticks to the script,' 'striking poses' that cannot be taken seriously.[10]

If the public escapes its marginalization and passivity, we face a 'crisis of democracy' that must be overcome, liberal intellectuals explain, in part through measures to discipline the institutions responsible for 'the indoctrination of the young' – schools, university, churches, and the like – and perhaps even government control of the media if self-censorship does not suffice. The American contributor to the report, Samuel Huntington, explained elsewhere that 'The architects of power in the United States must create a force that can be felt but not seen . . . Power remains strong when it remains in the dark; exposed to the sunlight it begins to evaporate.'[11]

In taking these views, contemporary intellectuals are drawing on good constitutional sources. James Madison held that power must be delegated to 'the wealth of the nation', 'the more capable set of men', who understand that the role of government is 'to protect the minority of the opulent against the majority'. Pre-capitalist in his world view, Madison had faith that the 'enlightened statesman' and 'benevolent philosopher' who were to exercise power would 'discern the true interest of their country' and guard the public interest against the 'mischief' of democratic majorities. The mischief would be avoided, Madison hoped, under the system of fragmentation he devised. In later years, he came to fear that severe problems would arise with the likely increase of those who 'will labor under all the hardships of life, and secretly sigh for a more equal distribution of its benefits' – sighs that must somehow be driven from the mind. A good deal of modern history reflects these conflicts over who will make decisions, and how.

Recognition that control of opinion is the foundation of government goes back at least to David Hume, who held that 'the maxim extends to the most despotic and military governments, as well as to the most free and most popular'. But a qualification should be added. It is far more important in the more free societies, where obedience cannot be maintained by the lash. It is only natural that the modern institutions of thought control – frankly called 'propaganda' before the word became unfashionable because of totalitarian associations – should have originated in the most free societies. Britain pioneered with its Ministry of Information: its 'task . . . was to direct the thought of most of the world', particularly of progressive intellectuals in the United States, whose own task was to drive a reluctant public to war and who later took great pride in having done so (they believed). Wilson followed soon after with his Committee on Public Information. Its propaganda successes inspired progressive democratic theorists and the modern public relations industry. Leading participants in the CPI, like Lippmann and Edward Bernays, quite explicitly drew from these achievements of thought control, the new 'art of democracy' that is the 'very essence of the democratic process'. The term 'propaganda' became an entry in the *Encyclopedia Britannica* in 1922, and in the *Encyclopedia of Social Sciences* a decade later, with Harold

Lasswell's scholarly endorsement of the new techniques for controlling the public mind. The methods of the pioneers were particularly significant, Randal Marlin writes in his history of propaganda, because of their 'widespread imitation . . . by Nazi Germany, South Africa, the Soviet Union, and the US Pentagon',[12] though the achievements of the PR industry dwarf them all.

Problems of 'population control', to borrow a phrase from counterinsurgency literature, become particularly severe when the governing authorities carry out policies that are opposed by the general public. In that case, the political leadership may be tempted to follow the path taken by the Reagan administration, which established an Office of Public Diplomacy to conduct such programs as Operation Truth to manufacture public consent for its murderous policies in Central America. One high government official described Operation Truth as 'a huge psychological operation of the kind the military conducts to influence a population in denied or enemy territory'[13] – a frank characterization of pervasive attitudes towards the domestic population.

Enemy Territory Abroad

While efforts to control enemy territory at home often have to rely on intensive propaganda campaigns, constraints are lifted beyond the borders, where more direct means are available. The leaders of the first of the two superpowers of the new millennium – mostly recycled from more reactionary sectors of the Reagan–Bush I administrations – provided vivid illustrations during their first twelve years in office. When the traditional regime of violence and repression was challenged by the Church and other miscreants in the Central American domains of US power, the Reagan administration responded with a 'war on terror', declared as soon as they took office in 1981. To the surprise of no one with historical memory, it instantly became a violent terrorist war, a campaign of slaughter, torture, and barbarism, extending to other regions of the world as well.

In one country, Nicaragua, Washington had lost control of the armed forces that had traditionally subdued the population of the region, one of the bitter legacies of Wilsonian idealism. The US-backed Somoza dictatorship was overthrown by the Sandinista rebels, and the murderous National Guard was dismantled. Therefore Nicaragua had to be subjected to a campaign of international terrorism that left the country ruined, facing a questionable future. Even the psychological effects of Washington's terrorist war are severe. The spirit of exuberance, vitality, and optimism after the overthrow of the dictatorship could not long survive as the reigning superpower intervened to dash the hopes that a grim history might finally take a different course.

In the other Central American countries targeted by the Reaganite 'war on terror', the armies installed, armed, and trained by the United States maintained control. The population did not have an army to defend it from the terrorists – that is, the security forces – so that atrocities were even worse. The record of mass murder, torture, and devastation was extensively reported by human rights organizations, church groups, Latin American scholars, and many others, but remained little known to citizens of the state that bore prime responsibility, and was quickly effaced.

Perhaps the most revealing indication of elite attitudes towards state-sponsored terror is the commentary at the critical extreme within the national media. Critics objected to Washington's terrorist war in Nicaragua as a 'clear failure' and urged that other means be found to restore Nicaragua to the 'Central American mode' of the US-backed states, and to compel it to conform to their 'regional standard'. The disobedient Nicaraguans must submit to a 'regional arrangement that would be enforced by Nicaragua's neighbors', who were then massacring, destroying, and torturing in a manner that would have impressed other Washington favorites of the day: Iraq's Saddam Hussein, Indonesia's Suharto, Romania's Ceausescu, and others of similar distinction.[14]

By the mid-1980s, the US-backed state terrorist campaigns had created societies 'affected by terror and panic . . . collective intimidation and generalized fear', in the words of a leading Church-based Salvadoran human rights organization: the population had 'internalized acceptance of . . . the daily and frequent use of violent means . . . the frequent appearance of tortured bodies'. Returning from a brief visit to his native Guatemala, journalist Julio Godoy wrote that 'one is tempted to believe that some people in the White House worship Aztec gods – with the offering of Central American blood'. He had fled a year earlier when his newspaper, *La Epoca*, was blown up by state terrorists, an operation that aroused no interest in the United States, just as when the same had happened in El Salvador: attention was carefully focused on the misdeeds of the official enemy, real no doubt, but hardly detectable in the context of US-backed state terror in the region.

The White House, Godoy wrote, installed and supported forces in Central America that 'can easily compete against Nicolae Ceaus. escu's Securitate for the World Cruelty Prize'.[15]

To people in the region, Godoy was saying nothing that they did not know from their own bitter lives, nor was it unfamiliar to those in the Western democracies who chose to know. But all is safely buried, thanks to the talents of the custodians of public consciousness.

After the terrorist commanders had achieved their goals, the consequences were reviewed at a conference in San Salvador of Jesuits and lay associates, who had more than enough personal experience to draw on, quite apart from what they had been observing through the grisly decade of the 1980s. The conference concluded that it does not suffice to focus on the terror alone, extraordinary as it was in brutality and scale. It is no less important 'to explore . . . what weight the culture of terror has had in domesticating the expectations of the majority vis-à-vis alternatives different to those of the powerful'.[16] Not only in Central America.

Once 'the Central American mode' was preserved by violence, and the 'culture of terror' properly established, attention can turn elsewhere. Meanwhile, the countries liberated under the Reaganite onslaught survive largely by remittances, while children sniff glue to relieve the hunger, beg for a pittance to survive the night, or are simply murdered by the thousands in Tegucigalpa, Guatemala City, and San Salvador, where the 'regional standards' were upheld throughout the 1980s in pursuit of 'America's mission'.[17]

Destroying hope is a critically important project. And

when it is achieved, formal democracy is allowed; even preferred, if only for public relations purposes. In more honest circles, much of this is conceded. Of course, it is understood much more profoundly by the beasts in men's shapes who endure the consequences of challenging the imperatives of stability and order.

These are all matters that the second superpower should make every effort to understand, if it hopes to escape the containment doctrines to which it is subjected, and to take seriously the ideals of justice and freedom that come easily to the lips but are harder to defend and advance.

Realities, 2004

The National Security Strategy (NSS) announced in
September 2002, and its immediate implementation in Iraq,
have been widely regarded as a watershed in international
affairs. 'The new approach is revolutionary,' Henry
Kissinger wrote.[1] It undermines the seventeenth-century
Westphalian system of international order, and of course
the UN Charter and international law. Kissinger approved
of the doctrine but with reservations about style and tactics,
and with a crucial qualification: it cannot be 'a universal
principle available to every nation'. Rather, the right of
aggression must be reserved to the United States, perhaps
delegated to chosen clients. We must forcefully reject the
most elementary of moral truisms: the principle of universality. Kissinger is to be praised for his honesty in forth-
rightly articulating prevailing doctrine, usually concealed
in professions of virtuous intent and tortured legalisms.

Arthur Schlesinger agreed that the doctrine and implementation were 'revolutionary', but for different reasons.
As the first bombs fell on Baghdad, he recalled Franklin
Delano Roosevelt's words when Japan bombed Pearl
Harbor on 'a date which will live in infamy'. Now it is
Americans who live in infamy, Schlesinger continued, as
their government adopts the policies of imperial Japan. He
added that George W. Bush had succeeded in converting
a 'global wave of sympathy' for the United States to
a 'global wave of hatred of American arrogance and

militarism'. A year later, not surprisingly, 'discontent with America and its policies ha[d] intensified rather than diminished', the Pew Research Center found. Even in Britain support for the war had declined by a third. And among Latin American elites – the most pro-US element in the region that has the longest experience with US policies – opposition to Bush reached 87 percent, 98 percent in Brazil, and almost as high in Mexico.[2]

As also anticipated, the war increased the threat of terror. Surveying attitudes in the Muslim world, Middle East expert Fawaz Gerges found that 'It's simply unbelievable how the war has revived the appeal of a global jihadi Islam that was in real decline after 9-11.' Recruitment for the al-Qaeda networks increased, reaching more 'menacing' sectors, while Iraq itself became a 'terrorist haven' for the first time, also suffering its first suicide attacks since the thirteenth century. Suicide attacks worldwide for the year 2003 reached the highest level in modern times.[3] Substantial specialist opinion believes that the war led to the proliferation of weapons of mass destruction (WMD), also as predicted.[4]

In the Mideast, Gerges reports, 'Far from empowering the democrats or the reformists, the war in Iraq has supplied more ammunition to militant elements and alienated moderate secular and Muslim public opinion.' The outcome 'is something deadlier than the worst scenario sketched by "liberal pessimists"', Mideast specialist Dilip Hiro writes: 'The Anglo-American invasion of Iraq has led to an alliance of Arab nationalism with Islamist militancy, a most powerful compound with serious implications for the rest of the Arab Middle East.'[5]

Blair, Bush, and company claimed that they had to invade

Iraq because its WMD and ties to terror posed an 'existential threat' – which they chose, deliberately, to intensify.

As the anniversary of the invasion approached, New York's Grand Central Station was patrolled by police with flak jackets and submachine guns, a reaction to the 11 March Madrid bombings that killed 200 people in Europe's worst terrorist crime. The year 2003 had ended with an unprecedented terror alert in the United States. Immediately after the Madrid bombing, Spain voted out the government that had gone to war against the will of an overwhelming majority. Spanish voters were bitterly condemned for appeasing terrorism by voting to withdraw troops from Iraq in the absence of UN authorization – that is, for adopting a position similar to that of Americans, 70 percent of whom say the UN should 'take the lead to work with Iraqis to write a new constitution and build a new democratic government', and since April 2003 had called for the UN to take the leading role in 'civil order and economic reconstruction' in Iraq. The US figures are particularly noteworthy in the light of the fact that popular opinion is scarcely reported, the views expressed receive little articulate support, and the issues do not appear on the electoral agenda; unlike Spain, in all of these respects. Still more noteworthy is that the views of Americans are held despite remarkable misperceptions about the war, probably unique in the world.[6]

Five months after he triumphantly declared victory in a carefully staged extravaganza on the aircraft carrier *Abraham Lincoln*, Bush assured the American people that 'The world is safer today because, in Iraq, our coalition ended a regime that cultivated ties to terror while it built weapons of mass destruction.'[7] Similar messages have regularly been produced since, for example, by National Security Adviser Condoleezza Rice in January 2004.[8] The president's handlers and speech writers know that every word is false, but they also know that the most outlandish lies can become Truth, if repeated loudly and insistently enough. Those with some concern about the future may prefer a more sober evaluation.

There is a broad consensus of specialist opinion on how to reduce the threat of terror – keeping here to the subcategory that is doctrinally acceptable, *their* terror against *us* – and also on how to incite further terrorist atrocities, which, sooner or later, may become truly horrendous: linking of terror and WMD is only a matter of time. The consensus is well articulated by Jason Burke in his study of the al-Qaeda phenomenon,[9] the most detailed and informed investigation of this loose array of radical Islamists, mostly by now independent, for whom bin Laden is hardly more than a symbol, and who may well be a more dangerous one after he is killed, becoming a martyr who will inspire others to join his cause. The role of the current incumbents, during their Reaganite phase, in creating the radical Islamist networks is well known. Less familiar is their tolerance of Pakistan's slide toward radical Islamist extremism under the rule of one of the many brutal dictators they supported, Zia al-Huq, and their willingness to look away while their ally was developing nuclear weapons; Reagan annually endorsed the pretense that Pakistan was not developing them, and his successors paid little attention while Pakistan's leading proliferator, now tapped on the wrist, was carrying out what appears to be the world's most extraordinary nuclear smuggling enterprise.[10]

As Burke reviews, bin Laden was created as a symbol, and al-Qaeda was virtually created as well, by Clinton's

1998 bombing of the Sudan and Afghanistan, which led to a sharp increase in support, recruitment, and financing for the virtually unknown al-Qaeda, and also forged close relations between bin Laden and the Taliban, previously cool or hostile.[11]

We might tarry at this point to look into the mirror, often a useful exercise. We learn a lot about Western civilization by observing the reaction to the bombing in Sudan, which led to tens of thousands of deaths according to the only credible estimates – perhaps less, perhaps more. It was known of course that the bombing would probably lead to a humanitarian catastrophe, as Human Rights Watch warned at once, giving good reasons. Investigations are sparse, and interest non-existent, apart from fury when the matter is raised. The reaction might be different if the major producer of pharmaceutical supplies had been destroyed by a terrorist attack in the United States, Canada, Israel, or some other place that matters.

The reaction in this case is conventional. No notice is taken when a prominent historian refers in passing to 'the elimination of hundreds of thousands of native people' in the conquest of the national territory. Imagine the reaction to a comparable reference in the German press to 'the elimination of hundreds of thousands of Jews'. Probably few would even understand why the comparison is apt.[12] The scale of deaths in Washington's Indochina wars is unknown within millions. Median judgments of Vietnamese deaths are a few percent of the official figures, let alone the actual ones. The effects of US chemical warfare in South Vietnam are of slight concern, apart from American soldiers – serious enough, but a minuscule fraction of what was suffered by South Vietnamese.

There is no interest in the discovery by Western scientists that use of highly carcinogenic dioxin was at twice the level reported, more than ten times the intensity of domestic use, with more than 600,000 victims according to Vietnamese studies, leaving hideously deformed fetuses in Saigon hospitals and children with horrible malformations, some born well after the crimes were stopped. We can be confident that the graphic account by one of the world's leading photojournalists will not be a best-seller among those responsible for the atrocity.[13]

The tenth anniversary of the Rwandan genocide has been marked by justified horror, not only about the events, but also the unwillingness of the West, Clinton in particular, to act to mitigate the slaughter – though that is far from the whole story. There are easy ways to test the depth and character of the concern. Every day, more than 3,000 children die in southern Africa from malaria, probably two or three times that many from other easily treatable diseases. It would cost pennies to save them. That is several 9-11s every day among children alone, just in Africa, economist Jeffrey Sachs writes, attempting to arouse concern about the slaughter. The Rwandan genocide, according to the official account, lasted about a hundred days. Simple arithmetic tells us that while lamenting the genocide, we watch a Rwanda-style massacre daily, and not just for a hundred days, while deploring our failure to act ten years ago. And this case is far easier to deal with. It requires only bribing pharmaceutical corporations, not sending troops. But it is our crime, easily preventable, going on every day, so it is off the agenda.[14]

Clients receive the same exemption from culpability or concern. In the first month of the current Intifada, the death toll was 4 Israelis and 75 Palestinians, many killed by US helicopters attacking civilian complexes. Clinton sent the largest shipment of new military helicopters in a decade as the first reports of their use appeared, but the press kept silent. Journalist Amira Hass has sought to compile the figures for the five months ending in February 2004. These are exact for Israelis, uncertain for those under military occupation. The IDF reports 27 Israeli civilians and 67 soldiers killed; the best estimate for Palestinians is 1,230. In the Gaza Strip, 940 Palestinians were killed, including 81 women and 344 children under the age of eighteen. Israel's 'targeted assassinations' killed 46 suspects and 80 passersby 'killed with "pinpoint prevention"'.[15]

Which ones register in the conscience of those who provide the arms and diplomatic support for the occupation?

Similarly, the scale of Iraqi casualties is unknown. A British medical group estimated the toll in the tens of thousands by November 2003, also reporting increase in maternal mortality rates and a near doubling of acute malnutrition along with increase in water-borne and vaccine-preventable diseases. Analysts recognized that the figures can be only 'informed guesswork', because the matter is too insignificant to investigate.[16]

The traditional victims often see the world somewhat differently.

After Clinton's 1998 bombings, the next major contribution to the growth of the al-Qaeda 'network of networks', and the prominence of bin Laden, was the bombing of Afghanistan, undertaken without credible pretext as later quietly conceded. As a result, '[T]he language of bin Laden and his concept of the cosmic struggle has now spread among tens of millions of people, particularly the young and angry, around the world,' Burke writes, reviewing the sharp increase in global terror and the creation of 'a whole new cadre of terrorists' enlisted in what they see as a 'titanic battle': the 'cosmic struggle between good and evil', the 'vision' shared by bin Laden and Bush. As noted, the invasion of Iraq had the same effect, as anticipated.

Reviewing many examples, Burke concludes that 'Every use of force is another small victory for bin Laden': thanks to Clinton and particularly Bush, bin Laden 'is winning', whether he lives or dies. Burke's general conclusions are widely shared by many analysts, including former heads of Israeli military intelligence and the General Security Services (Shin Bet).[17]

New illustrations are recorded regularly. Thus, on 22 March 2004, Israel assassinated the quadriplegic Sheikh Ahmed Yassin, a revered figure considered by serious analysts to be one of the more conciliatory figures in the Hamas leadership.[18] That set off the anticipated furious reaction in the region, including massive demonstrations and protest in Iraq. A week later, four US security contractors were murdered in Fallujah, their corpses desecrated by the mob. Responsibility was taken by the previously unknown 'Brigades of Martyr Ahmed Yassin', who issued a statement calling the murders 'a gift from the people of Fallujah to the people of Palestine and the family of Sheikh Ahmed Yassin who was assassinated by the criminal Zionists' – using a US helicopter sent to them with the foreknowledge that it will be used for such purposes. That led to a murderous assault by US marines, killing hundreds of people and contributing to a sudden spread of violence throughout much of Iraq that for the first time united Sunni and Shi'ite resistance to the occupying army.[19]

Once again, Ariel Sharon has demonstrated that his arm is long, with Washington's assistance. The Yassin assassination was another 'victory for bin Laden', and for those on all sides who are yearning for a 'cosmic struggle'.

There is also a broad consensus on the proper reaction to terror, at least on the part of those who prefer to reduce the threat rather than to strike heroic poses. It is two-pronged: directed at the terrorists themselves, and at the reservoir of potential support. The terrorists see themselves as a vanguard, seeking to mobilize others. The appropriate response to their actions is police work, which has been successful, in Germany, Indonesia, Pakistan, and elsewhere. That includes cutback of financing, which has also been successful, though it is no simple task. US counter-terrorism specialists report that they knew well that IRA terror was financed in the United States, sometimes indirectly through collections in churches, but did not stop it and doubt that they could have, though such measures are now being demanded of Saudi Arabia, and substantially carried out, it appears.[20]

More important is the broad constituency the vanguard is seeking to reach, including people who may fear and even hate them but nevertheless see them as fighting for a cause that is right and just. This is a potential reservoir of support that we can choose to mobilize by violence, or can support along constructive paths by addressing the 'myriad grievances', many quite legitimate, that are 'the root causes of modern Islamic militancy', Burke writes. 'A first line of defense,' against terror, Atran adds, 'is to understand and act on the root causes of terrorism to reduce drastically the receptivity of potential recruits to the message and methods of terror-sponsoring organizations, mostly through political, economic, and social action programs . . . The basis of community support for organizations that sponsor terrorism needs to be the prime long-term focus of US policymakers and others who are interested in combating the threat such organizations pose.' That requires 'denying support to discredited governments and making maximum efforts to end the conflict in the Palestinian territories, whose daily images of violence engender global Muslim resentment'.[21] Efforts such as these can significantly reduce the threat of terror, and should be undertaken independently of this goal.

Violence can succeed, as we know very well from the conquest of the national territory. But at terrible cost. It can also provoke greater violence in response, and often does. Inciting terror is not the only case. Others are even more hazardous.

In February 2004, Russia carried out its largest military exercises in two decades, prominently exhibiting advanced WMD. General Baluyevsky informed the press that the Americans 'are trying to make nuclear weapons an instrument of solving military tasks, [to] lower the threshold of nuclear weapons use. Shouldn't we react to that . . . ? I'm sure that we should, and we are doing that.' He cited Bush administration plans to develop low-yield nuclear weapons. That is 'an extremely dangerous tendency that is undermining global and regional stability', Russian Defense Minister Sergei Ivanov and his associates warned, 'lowering the threshold for actual use'. Russia can scarcely be unaware that the new 'bunker busters' are designed to target the high-level nuclear command bunkers, hidden inside mountains, that control their nuclear arsenal (strategic analyst Bruce Blair). Ivanov warned further that 'American development of new types of nuclear weapons, armed actions that bypass the UN Security Council and anti-Russian attitudes inside NATO, could force his nation to adopt tougher defense measures' – meaning offensive weapons. Ivanov and Russian generals report that they will match US escalation of nuclear and other offensive forces, and that they are now deploying 'the most advanced state-of-the-art missile in the world', perhaps systems that would be next to impossible to destroy, which 'would be very alarming to the Pentagon', former Assistant Defense Secretary Phil Coyle says.

US analysts suspect that Russia may also be duplicating US development of a hypersonic Cruise Vehicle that can re-enter the atmosphere from space and launch devastating attacks on command bunkers and other targets without warning, part of US plans to reduce reliance on overseas bases or the need to negotiate access to air routes.[22]

US analysts estimate that Russian military expenditures may have tripled during the Bush–Putin years, in large measure a predicted reaction to Bush administration militancy and aggressiveness. Putin and Ivanov indicated that they too would adopt the Bush doctrine of 'preemptive strike', meaning aggression at will – the 'revolutionary' new doctrine of the NSS. They also 'added a key detail, saying that military force can be used if there is an attempt to limit Russia's access to regions that are essential to its survival', thus adopting the Clinton doctrine that the US is entitled to resort to 'unilateral use of military power' to ensure 'uninhibited access to key markets, energy supplies and strategic resources'. Russia also 'moved to make dozens of previously stored multi-warhead SS-19 ICBMs combat-ready'.[23]

The world 'is a much more insecure place' now that Russia has decided to follow the US lead, said Fiona Hill, Russia scholar and senior fellow at the Brookings Institution: 'You can't expect to reserve that right exclusively for yourself.' Now, 'the cat is out of the bag . . . The Russians are following suit, and presumably other countries will follow suit.'[24]

These reactions to US militancy pose an enormous threat to the United States, and the world. In the past, Russian automated response systems have come within a few minutes of launching a nuclear strike, barely aborted by human intervention. By now the systems have deteriorated. US systems allow three minutes for human judgment after computers warn of a missile attack, a regular event, followed by a thirty-second presidential briefing. The Pentagon has also found serious flaws in computer security systems, which might allow terrorist hackers to seize control and simulate a launch – 'an accident waiting to happen', Blair writes.[25] The dangers are being consciously escalated by the threat and use of violence.

Concern is not eased by the recent discovery that US presidents have been 'systematically misinformed' about the effects of nuclear war, with the level of destruction 'severely underestimated' because of lack of systematic oversight of the 'insulated bureaucracies' that provide analyses of 'limited and "winnable" nuclear war', leading to 'institutional myopia [that] can be catastrophic',[26] much more so than failures and manipulation of intelligence on Iraq.

The Bush administration announced deployment of the

first stages of a missile defense system in summer 2004. This was criticized as a 'completely political' gesture employing untested technology at huge expense.[27] A more appropriate criticism is that the system might work, or at least look as if it might; in the logic of nuclear war, what counts is perception, not reality. US planners and potential targets agree that missile defense is a first-strike weapon, intended to provide more freedom for aggression. And they know how the United States responded to Russia's deployment of a very limited ABM system in 1968: by targeting it with nuclear weapons to ensure that any defense would be instantly overwhelmed. Reviewing recently declassified records on the US response, strategic analysts warn that current US plans will not only provoke a Russian response but a more significant Chinese reaction, since 'the credibility of its nuclear retaliatory deterrent will be fundamentally challenged'. History and the logic of deterrence 'remind us that missile defense systems are potent drivers of offensive nuclear planning', and the Bush initiative will be no different, again raising the threat to Americans and to the world.[28]

China's predicted reaction may set off a ripple effect through India, Pakistan, and beyond. Less discussed, but no less important, is the threat emanating from West Asia. Israel's nuclear capacities, far beyond any regional power and complemented by other WMD, are described as 'dangerous in the extreme' by the former head of the US Strategic Command, General Lee Butler, not only because of the threat they pose but also because they stimulate proliferation. The United States is now increasing the threat. Israel's air force is already larger and technologically more advanced than that of any NATO power (the

US excepted), according to IDF analysts. Washington is now providing the IDF air force with more than a hundred advanced jet bombers, F-16I's, for which there is no credible defensive need. This is the biggest purchase in the history of the state. The dispatch of these planes is accompanied by prominent announcements that the planes can reach Iran and return, and that they are an advanced version of the US planes that Israel used to destroy Iraq's nuclear reactor in 1981 – an attack commonly depicted as having inhibited Saddam Hussein's nuclear weapons program, though it was known almost at once, and has since been confirmed, that the attack led to the *initiation* of a serious nuclear weapons program, in the usual cycle of violence provoking more extreme violence. The Israeli press adds further that the United States is providing the IDF air force with '"special" weaponry' ('himush "myuhad"'). Though these 'secret leaks' are restricted to the Hebrew press, there can be little doubt that Iranian and other intelligence services are watching closely, and probably giving a worst-case analysis: that these might be nuclear weapons. The leaks and the provision of F-16Is may be intended to rattle the Iranian leadership, perhaps to provoke them to some action that can be used as a pretext for an attack.[29]

The 'revolutionary' NSS was formally announced along with the virtual declaration of war against Iraq and the instructions to the Security Council that they could be 'relevant' by endorsing what the United States would do anyway, or be a debating society. To be taken seriously, and to be soberly portrayed by specialists as a 'new norm in international relations', a doctrine must be implemented. The most prominent implementation was the invasion of Iraq. Much less publicized but perhaps more ominous was the immediate acceleration of the aggressive military posture. The United States moved at once to terminate negotiations on an enforceable bioweapons treaty, and to block international efforts to ban biowarfare and militarization of space, in the latter case adopting the stance that had paralyzed the UN disarmament commission during the Clinton years. The Air Force Space Command at once announced far-reaching programs to move from *'control'* of space, which *'means superiority in information and significant force enhancement'*, to *'ownership'* of space, which *'may mean instant engagement anywhere in the world'* – putting any part of the world at risk of instant destruction, thanks to sophisticated global surveillance and lethal offensive weaponry in space.[30]

A year later, at the UN General Assembly meetings in fall 2003, the United States voted alone against implementation of the Comprehensive Test Ban Treaty and alone with its new ally India against steps toward the total elimination of nuclear weapons. The United States voted alone against 'observance of environmental norms in the drafting and implementation of disarmament and arms control agreements', and voted alone with Israel and Micronesia against steps to prevent nuclear proliferation in the Middle East – the pretext for invading Iraq. A resolution to prevent militarization of space passed 174 to 0, with 4 abstentions: the United States, Israel, Micronesia, Marshall Islands.[31] A negative US vote or abstention amounts to a double veto: the resolution is blocked, and is eliminated from reporting and history.

Bush planners know as well as others that the resort to force and their militaristic and aggressive posture increase the threat of terror and the risk of catastrophe. They do not desire these outcomes, but assign them low priority in comparison to the international and domestic agendas they make little attempt to conceal.

The NSS has ample precedents, going back to the early days of World War II. But Kissinger was right to call it 'revolutionary', not so much in content as in style and implementation. It elicited unprecedented popular protest around the world, including economic and foreign policy elites, at home as well. The main establishment journal, *Foreign Affairs*, at once criticized this 'new imperial grand strategy' as a danger to the United States and the world. Others agreed, across a broad range. But the criticism, rather like Kissinger's, was on narrow grounds. As Clinton's Secretary of State Madeleine Albright explained in *Foreign Affairs*, every administration has a similar doctrine, but it is 'quietly held in reserve', to be used when needed. It is a mistake to smash the world in the face with brazen arrogance, and to implement the doctrine in ways that arouse antagonism and countermeasures that could be harmful to the interests protected by Washington.

The critique of the doctrines and implementation is indeed unprecedented, but the broad acceptance of their fundamental principles is also important to understand. At the extreme, the respected analyst Andrew Bacevich regards the spectrum as so narrow that politics should be dismissed with ridicule. In a perceptive analysis of the extremism and near unanimity of the bipartisan consensus, Stephen Zunes analyzes its import for the Middle East region. Chalmers Johnson's critique takes a broader and grimmer view, interpreting it as part of a drift toward militarism and imperialism that signals an end to the 'constitutional republic', with worse to come.[32] Whatever one's assessment may be, the stakes are not slight.

The NSS declared that Washington has a 'sovereign right to use force to defend ourselves' from nations that possess WMD and cooperate with terrorists, Colin Powell's defense of the doctrine before a hostile audience at the World Economic Forum. As constantly stressed by Powell and his British counterparts, the 'single question' was the one posed by the president: 'Has the Iraqi regime fully and unconditionally disarmed as required by [UN Security Council Resolution] 1441, or has it not?' Bush and associates also made it clear that ridding the country of Saddam Hussein was not the issue: thus at the Summit meeting on the eve of the invasion, they announced that the United States and United Kingdom would invade even if Saddam and his family left the country.[33]

The collapse of the official pretexts is well known.[34] But there has been insufficient attention to its most important consequence: the NSS was effectively revised to lower the bars to aggression. The need to establish ties to terror was quietly dropped. More significantly, Bush and colleagues now declare the right to resort to force even if a country does not have WMD or even programs to develop them. It is sufficient that it has the 'intent and ability' to do so. Just about every country has the ability. And intent is in the eye of the beholder. The official doctrine, then, is that anyone is subject to overwhelming attack, if we so decide. No pretexts are necessary. Colin Powell carried the revision even a step farther. The president had to attack Iraq in self-defense because Saddam not only had 'intent and capability' but 'actually used such horrible weapons against their enemies in Iran and against their own people' – with continuing support from the current incumbents, including him, he failed to add, following the usual convention.

In Condoleezza Rice's version, the invasion was necessary because Saddam 'had used weapons of mass destruction' (with continuing US support), 'had attacked his neighbors twice' (once with US support, the other time followed by US authorization to crush a rebellion that might have overthrown him), 'was allowing terrorists to run in his country and was funding terrorists outside of his country' (charges that remain higher truths despite lack of evidence), and had refused to account for his WMD and attempted to conceal his programs (so, *a fortiori*, we must attack Israel). With such reasoning as this, who is exempt from attack?[35]

Small wonder that 'If Iraqis ever see Saddam Hussein in the dock, they want his former American allies shackled beside him.'[36] That inconceivable event would be a radical revision of the fundamental principle of international tribunals: they must be restricted to the crimes of others.

In the desperate flailing to contrive justifications as one pretext after another collapses, the obvious reason for the invasion is conspicuously evaded: establishing the first stable military bases in an obedient client state right at the heart of the world's major energy resources, the 'stupendous source of strategic power' and incomparable 'material prize' identified by the State Department sixty years ago, and understood ever since to be a primary lever of world control, expected to become more important in the future. There should have been little surprise at revelations that the administration intended to attack Iraq before 9-11, and downgraded the 'war on terror' in favor of this objective. In comparison to the benefits of controlling Iraq, terror is a marginal issue, and even predictably increasing the threat is not a serious concern.

The convention of evasion does not extend to internal discussion, however. Long before, the private club of the reactionary statists in charge had recognized that 'the need for a substantial American force presence in the Gulf transcends the issue of the regime of Saddam Hussein'.[37] With all the vacillations of policy since the current incumbents and their mentors first took office in 1981, one guiding principle remains stable: Iraqis must not rule Iraq.

The NSS was only one component of the 'Bush doctrine'. A second was that 'Those who harbor terrorists are as guilty as the terrorists themselves,' and must be attacked and destroyed. Like the other component, this was a corollary to the principle that 'our responsibility to history' is 'to rid the world of evil'.[38] And it too is taken very seriously. The prominent strategic analyst Graham Allison regards it as the most important element of the Bush doctrine. In declaring that 'those who harbor terrorists are as guilty as the terrorists themselves' when announcing the invasion of Afghanistan (because of its refusal to hand over bin Laden without evidence), he writes, Bush 'unilaterally revoked the sovereignty of states that provide sanctuary to terrorists'. The doctrine has 'already become a de facto rule of international relations'.[39]

Allison and others do not add that they are calling for the bombing of the United States. By the narrowest definition of the term, the United States surely 'harbors terrorists'. The most glaring example, perhaps, is Orlando Bosch, one of the most notorious international terrorists, charged by the FBI with dozens of terrorist acts, some on US soil. He was granted a presidential pardon by Bush I after the Justice Department had called for his deportation on grounds of national security. The aftermath is highly instructive. Recognizing that the United States would not act to inhibit planning and implementation of terrorist crimes in Florida, Cuban intelligence infiltrated the terrorist groups, and in 1998, provided high officials of the FBI with voluminous documentary evidence, written and taped, of terrorist activities on US soil. The FBI responded: by arresting the Cubans who had provided the evidence. They were given heavy sentences, three for life, after a mock trial in Miami. Their appeal in March 2004 aroused as little attention as the events themselves. There are many other illustrations, some relating crucially to events right on the front pages at the same time, notably the case of Emmanuel Constant, founder of the FRAPH paramilitary forces that had prime responsibility for the murder of thousands of Haitians in the early 1990s under the military junta that was supported, not so tacitly, by Bush I and Clinton, and were again rampaging in early 2004 as the United States helped implement the overthrow of the democratic government in an eerie replay of what happened in 1991. Extradition requests for Constant were routinely ignored – perhaps, as commonly assumed, because he would reveal his contacts with the US government during his terrorist career.[40] There are many other examples, even keeping within the doctrinal bounds of what constitutes 'terrorism'.

True, all such cases are irrelevant, because they presuppose the principle of universality, and it is a central doctrine of the intellectual and political culture that moral truisms must be forcefully rejected, much as Kissinger emphasized, and any appeal to them bitterly condemned.

Presidents commonly have 'doctrines', but Bush II is the first to have 'visions' as well, possibly because his handlers recall the criticism of his father as lacking 'the vision thing'.

It has become a journalistic convention that references to Bush should hail his 'vision', suitably vague but inspiring. The most exalted of these visions, conjured up after all pretexts for invasion of Iraq had to be abandoned, was the vision of bringing democracy to Iraq and the Middle East. By August 2003, it was observed that 'As the search for illegal weapons in Iraq continues without success, the Bush administration has moved to emphasize a different rationale for the war against Saddam Hussein: using Iraq as the 'linchpin' to transform the Middle East and thereby reduce the terrorist threat to the United States.' By November the new vision had become the real truth about the war. David Ignatius, veteran *Washington Post* correspondent/commentator and former executive editor of the *International Herald Tribune*, wrote that 'this may be the most idealistic war fought in modern times – a war whose only coherent rationale, for all the misleading hype about weapons of mass destruction and al-Qaeda terrorists, is that it toppled a tyrant and created the possibility of a democratic future'. The president affirmed the vision in a widely lauded address a few days later.[41]

Responses ranged from rapturous awe to critical commentary, which praised the nobility and generosity of the vision but warned that it may be beyond our means: the beneficiaries may be too backward, we might be over-reaching, it might prove too costly. That this has been the guiding vision is presupposed throughout as self-evident. News stories open by reporting that 'The American project to build a stable democracy in Iraq has encountered many obstacles.' Commentators wonder whether 'today's pseudo-Wilsonian campaign to make the Middle East safe for democracy' can really succeed, and discuss the decline in influence of the idealistic neocons who have sought to base policy on 'American values' (presumably, freedom, rights, justice) rather than on a sober calculation of 'national interests'. Even the harshest critics of the neocons concede that they had at least 'had a vision', and that their 'decision to wage preemptive war in order to depose Saddam Hussein and trigger a democratic revolution across the Arab world has shaken the international system to its core'.[42] With considerable search, I have yet to find an exception.

What is the evidence for the assumption that these lofty goals inspire policy, or ever did? Examination reveals that it virtually reduces to declarations of leaders. But it is the merest truism that declarations of virtuous intent by political leaders carry no information, because they are entirely predictable. The rhetoric of Japanese fascists, Hitler, Stalin, and others like them was hailed by their acolytes as noble and generous, as it was, but we rightly attend to their practice, and have only contempt for the apologists. The reasons for dismissing the pronouncements happen to be unusually strong in the present case. To take them seriously, we must assume that our leaders are accomplished liars; while beating the war drums, they were declaring, loud and clear, that the reasons were entirely different. And if they were lying before their pretexts collapsed, it is the merest sanity to disregard what is produced to replace them.

Beyond pronouncement, there is ample relevant evidence – namely, of their contempt for democracy. The record is not just consistent past practice, though that is compelling enough. It was demonstrated with extraordinary clarity during the build-up to the war, as countries were assigned to the categories 'Old Europe', to be condemned, or 'New

Europe', the grand hope of the future. The criterion was precise: Old Europe is the governments that took the position of the overwhelming majority of their populations, whereas in New Europe governments overrode even larger popular majorities and followed orders from Crawford, Texas, thereby demonstrating their 'democratic credentials'. It is hard to think of a case in history where visceral hatred for democracy was expressed with such brazen clarity. The most striking example was Turkey, where the government decided to go along with the wishes of 95 percent of the population, and was bitterly condemned and warned of severe punishment. The most extreme stand was taken by Paul Wolfowitz, who berated the Turkish military for not compelling the government to serve Washington, and demanded that they apologize for this bad behavior and recognize that the duty of Turkey is to help America.

Wolfowitz's performance is particularly enlightening because he is cast as the visionary leading the noble crusade for democracy and rights. Ignatius's acclaim for our nobility, quoted earlier, was inspired by 'a classic Paul Wolfowitz moment' in Hilla, Iraq, where Wolfowitz quoted 'de Tocqueville's theories about democracy' and called on Iraqis to 'build democracy' – which doubtless impressed the audience at the site of the first well-substantiated massacre of civilians by US forces.[43] Wolfowitz is 'the paradigmatic figure of the war', Ignatius explained, 'and the Bush administration's idealist in chief'. He was concerned that Wolfowitz might be 'too idealistic – that his passion for the noble goals of the Iraq war might overwhelm the prudence and pragmatism that normally guide war planners'. But he was reassured by the 'genuine intellectual' who studies the Arab world deeply, 'bleeds for its oppression and dreams of liberating it' along with other suffering people who need our help. Still, 'the idealism of a Wolfowitz must be tempered by some very hard-headed judgments about how to protect US interests', Ignatius advises, joining others who inform us that American foreign policy has entered a 'noble phase' with a 'saintly glow', but warn that by 'granting idealism a near exclusive hold on our foreign policy' we might neglect our own interests in dedicated service to others.[44]

Wolfowitz has often demonstrated his passion for democracy. And it turns out that the example of Turkey, just mentioned, is not uncharacteristic. He has also had ample opportunity to reveal how his heart bleeds for suffering people, for example, when he served as Reagan's ambassador to Indonesia, under the rule of one of the most appalling mass murderers, torturers, and aggressors of the late twentieth century – while, on the side, gaining 'the dubious title of being the most corrupt world leader in recent history', a 'clear winner, according to British-based Transparency International', having amassed a family fortune 'estimated at anything between 15 billion and 35 billion US dollars', far outstripping second-place Marcos and third-place Mobutu,[45] also members in good standing of the Rogues Gallery of the administrations in which Wolfowitz served.

Wolfowitz was an enthusiastic advocate for Suharto, not only during his tenure as ambassador but also in later years. In May 1997, only a few months before the monster was overthrown from within, Wolfowitz informed Congress that 'any balanced judgment of the situation in Indonesia today, including the very important and sensitive issue of human rights, needs to take account of the significant progress that Indonesia has already made and needs to acknowledge that much of this progress has to be credited to the strong and remarkable leadership of president Suharto'. The same could have been said about Saddam Hussein while he was receiving the strong support of the Reagan–Bush administrations in which Wolfowitz served. Later Wolfowitz was to praise General Wiranto, who bears major responsibility for the final paroxysm of US/UK-backed Indonesian atrocities in East Timor in 1999. After the October 2002 Bali bombings, Wolfowitz informed a defense forum that 'the reason the terrorists are successful in Indonesia is because the Suharto regime fell and the methods that were used to suppress them are gone' – the methods that had left a hideous trail of corpses, tortured political prisoners, and ruined lands in East Timor, West Papua, and Aceh, not to speak of the army's role in fomenting communal violence within Indonesia. Australian international relations specialist Scott Burchill observes that Wolfowitz's praise for Suharto's methods offered a pretext for restoring full US military ties with Indonesia, retained throughout the years when its military commanders compiled an exemplary record of state terrorist crimes and aggression; or to turn to the Wolfowitz version, the Indonesian officers trained by the United States by and large 'have a much more modern outlook, a much more democratic outlook, and they'll be much more supportive of what Indonesia needs to have in terms of democracy'.[46]

Before he was sent to Indonesia, Wolfowitz was in charge of East Asian affairs at Reagan's State Department, where he watched over other brutal dictators, among them Marcos in the Philippines and Chun Doo-Hwan in South Korea, both supported by the Reagan administration until virtually the last moment, when it became clear that they would be overthrown from within.

The history is now being 'purified' to provide a more satisfactory US role alongside the courageous Asian democrats who finally rid their countries of the US-backed tyrannies. During the first Reagan administration, Wolfowitz was also responsible for killing a Chinese initiative to broker US–North Korean talks, 'a pretty creative and useful suggestion', according to veteran State Department China diplomat Charles Freeman; Wolfowitz even edited the Chinese proposal out of a cable sent by the US Embassy in Beijing to Washington, apparently out of ideological fanaticism.[47]

Wolfowitz's dedication to democracy and markets was revealed again after the invasion, when he issued his Determination and Findings (5 December 2003) on contracts for reconstruction. 'It is necessary for the protection of the essential security interests of the United States,' he determined, that competition for prime contracts for reconstruction exclude all countries that did not follow US orders. The phrase 'security' has its usual meaning, rather as in the 'national security exceptions' of the US-guided 'trade agreements', which permit both the United States and Haiti to rely on the dynamic state sector to socialize the risk and cost of the next phase of the economy under the pretext of 'defense', without violating sacred market principles. Halliburton, Bechtel, J. P. Morgan, and other supplicants will therefore have to face competition for contracts from Rwanda and the Solomon Islands, but not France, Germany, and Russia, with any costs incurred by these market-friendly procedures borne by the US taxpayer.

There is one particle of (apparent) evidence in support of the new vision: the invasion did depose Saddam Hussein, an outcome that can be welcomed without hypocrisy by those who strenuously opposed US–UK support for Saddam Hussein through his worst crimes, including the crushing of the Shi'ite rebellion that might have overthrown him. The reasons for that stance were frankly explained: the United States preferred a military junta that would rule the country with an 'iron fist' just as Saddam had done, and if 'the best of all worlds' – an iron-fisted junta without Saddam – is unavailable, then he would have to do, because Washington and its allies held the 'strikingly unanimous view' that 'whatever the sins of the Iraqi leader, he offered the West and the region a better hope for his country's stability than did those who have suffered his repression'. Those who believe that there has been a miraculous religious conversion in that regard may want to explain why they do not also accept Saddam's professions that he is a nice guy now, so that his past mistakes can be overlooked.

The end of Saddam's rule was one of two very welcome 'regime changes'. The other was the formal end of the murderous sanctions regime,[48] which killed hundreds of thousands of people by conservative estimate, devastating the civilian society, strengthening the tyrant, and compelling the population to rely on him for survival. It is because of these hideous consequences that the highly respected international diplomats who administered the programs, Denis Halliday and Hans von Sponeck, resigned in protest at what Halliday called the 'genocidal' sanctions regime. They are the Westerners who knew Iraq best, having access to regular information from a great many investigators in all parts of the country. The sanctions regime was administered by the UN, but its cruel and savage character was dictated by the United States and its British subordinate, which is why it is systematically excluded from discussion. Ending this regime is a very positive aspect of the invasion. But of course that could have been done, and sanctions could have been directed to weapons programs instead, without an invasion. So this beneficial consequence provides no justification for the invasion.

There is reason to believe – as Halliday and von Sponeck had argued – that if the vicious sanctions regime had been directed to preventing weapons programs, the population of Iraq would have been able to send Saddam Hussein to the same fate as other murderous gangsters supported by the current incumbents and their British allies: Ceausescu, Suharto, Marcos, Duvalier, Chun, Mobutu . . . – an impressive list, some of them comparable to Saddam, to which new names are being added daily by the same Western leaders. If so, both murderous regimes could have been ended without invasion. Postwar inquiries, such as those of Washington's Iraq Survey Group headed by David Kay, add weight to these beliefs by revealing how shaky Saddam's control of the country was in the last few years.

We may have our own subjective judgments about the matter, but elementary honesty dictates that they are completely irrelevant. Unless the population is given the opportunity to overthrow a brutal tyrant, as they did in the case of the other members of the Rogue's Gallery supported by the United States and United Kingdom, there is no justification for resort to outside force to do so. Another truism, which has repeatedly been pointed out – and systematically ignored within the doctrinal system.

That is sufficient to eliminate the particle of truth that might be adduced to support the new doctrine contrived after the collapse of the official reasons for invasion. On different grounds, these arguments have been thoroughly refuted by Human Rights Watch.[49] But there are many further considerations as well, some already mentioned.

In the face of these facts it would be surprising if *anyone* were to take seriously the professions of virtuous intent, and it is instructive that the commitment to do so appears to be exceptionless. Almost. I did find one exception, a news report in the *Washington Post* a few days after the president's proclamation of his vision to bring democracy to Iraq and beyond. The report presented the results of a Gallup poll in Baghdad, asking about motives for the US invasion. Some agreed with articulate opinion among the invaders that the goal was to establish democracy: 1 percent. Five percent felt that the goal was 'to assist the Iraqi people'. The rest assumed that the goal was to take control of Iraq's resources and to reorganize the Middle East in US and Israeli interests, or to get rid of Saddam Hussein for US purposes[50] – the possibility excluded in US commentary.

The results were in fact more nuanced. Though only 1 percent of Baghdadis thought the United States invaded to bring democracy, half felt that the United States wants democracy. A contradiction? Not really. The full response is that the United States wants to establish a democratic government, but 'would not allow Iraqis to do that without US pressure and influence'. In brief, democracy is fine, but only if you do what we say. They understand us better than we choose to understand ourselves: *choose*, because we have overwhelming evidence, if we are willing to look at it. In situations of dominance quite generally, those at the wrong end of the club tend to have clearer perceptions of reality.

US commentators like to see themselves as 'yearning for democracy', pursuing 'Wilsonian visions', etc., deterred from these noble goals by the Cold War, the ingratitude of their beneficiaries, naiveté and mistakes, terror, etc. The reality is frankly described by honest observers, including prominent scholars who have taken part in carrying out the 'vision', but recognize that the United States 'sincerely' wanted democracy only if it could be restricted to 'top-down forms of democracy' with traditional elites in power that are responsive to US demands (Thomas Carothers).

The highly consistent pattern was illustrated right on the front pages as the war's anniversary approached: the coup in Haiti. To sketch the immediately relevant background, in 1990 Haiti had its first free election. Remote from Western eyes, a vibrant and lively civil society had been organized in the slums and the hills, enabling the vast majority of the population to elect their own candidate, a populist priest, over enormous odds. Washington was appalled, and moved at once to undermine the democratic government. When it was overthrown by a military coup a few months later, Bush I and Clinton effectively supported the military junta and its wealthy supporters, even authorizing the Texaco oil company to supply them with oil in violation of presidential directives, thus rendering the OAS blockade that the United States had been openly undermining almost entirely meaningless. After three years of state violence, Clinton allowed President Aristide to return, but on a crucial condition: that he adopt the program of the defeated US candidate in the 1990 election, who won 14 percent of the vote – what we call 'restoring democracy' in an altruistic effort at 'nation building'. As predicted, the harsh neoliberal program imposed on Haiti undermined what was left of economic sovereignty, and drove the country into chaos and violence, accelerated by Bush's banning of international aid on cynical grounds.[51] By focusing on the final days, reporting and commentary were able to evade the uncomfortable truths and what they reveal, keeping to distribution of blame among Haitians in their 'failed state'.

During the first modern democratic revolution, in seventeenth-century England, the pamphlets of the popular democratic forces declared that they did not want to be ruled by 'knights and gentlemen . . . that are chosen for fear and do but oppress us', but 'by countrymen like ourselves, that know our wants' and do 'know the people's sores'. That has happened in Latin America: in Haiti, more recently in Brazil, though the 'knights and gentlemen' have constructed institutional means to ensure that the people's sores will not be tended. Such democratic achievements are next to inconceivable in the United States, a fact that might suggest some reflection on the fashionable notions 'failed state' and 'nation building'.

The program that Clinton imposed on Aristide is approximately the same as the one dictated by Pentagon proconsul Paul Bremer for Iraq, Order 39, allowing effective takeover of the economy by foreign banks and businesses. It is a sound conclusion of economic history that such measures, undermining economic sovereignty, also undermine development and reduce political democracy to a shadow. In fact, these are the kinds of programs that helped create the 'third world', where they were imposed by force, while the imperial powers resorted to radical state intervention to protect the rich from market discipline, as they still do, the United States very prominently among them from its origins until today.

In the same days in March 2004, the standard pattern was also illustrated in an election in El Salvador. To ensure that the democratic vote would come out the right way, the Bush administration warned that if it did not, the country's lifeline – remittances from the United States, a crucial pillar of the 'economic miracle' – might be cut, along with other consequences familiar to the population.[52] Keeping to convention, these moves to undermine democratic elections were interpreted as part of the crusade to bring democracy to a world that pleads for our assistance. Salvadorans too young to recall what the warnings mean may look across the border to Nicaragua. After the Reagan–Bush terrorist war of the 1980s, the population accepted the US candidate, only to find that their punishment did not end. Since the United States took over again, the country has declined to second poorest in the hemisphere, after Haiti. According to current Health Ministry reports, 60 percent of children under two are suffering from anemia due to malnutrition caused by severe poverty, with likely mental retardation. Quite a change from twenty years earlier, when Washington was panicked by reports from UNICEF, the World Bank, and other international agencies about Nicaragua's 'remarkable' achievements that were 'laying a solid foundation for long-term socio-economic development' as the country enjoyed 'one of the most dramatic improvements in child survival in the developing world'.[53]

The costs of seeking independence are not slight, and the fanaticism of those determined to prevent it can be quite extraordinary, even reaching to punishment for American scientists who dare to edit journal submissions from Cuba or try to attend medical conferences there,[54]

the latter particularly threatening because of embarrass-
ment that health outcomes in a poor country that has been
under US terrorist attack and illegal economic embargo
for forty-five years are about the same as in the United
States.

Iraqis do not have to know US history to draw conclusions about the noble vision. Their own history suffices.
Iraq was created by the British with boundaries to ensure
that Britain would gain the oil reserves of the north, not
Turkey, and that Iraq would be virtually barred from the
sea by the British colony of Kuwait. Iraq was 'independent', with a constitution and other forms of parliamentary
government. Iraqis did not have to read classified British
foreign office documents to understand that Britain
intended to impose an 'Arab façade' while Britain would
rule behind various 'constitutional fictions'.

Furthermore, they can see what is happening before
their eyes. Iraqis do not have to read the US press to discover
that 'Even after the transfer of power, US officials said they
plan a huge military and diplomatic presence in the independent Iraq. "The coalition authority will become the
world's largest embassy America has," Bremer said last
night, adding that the embassy would employ "thousands"
of US officials.' More than 3,000 personnel, according to
the State Department, 'the largest diplomatic staff anywhere
in the world' – not in order to supervise transfer of mean-
ingful sovereignty to Iraqis. And Iraqis would be hardly
surprised to learn that US officials intend 'to postpone some
[Iraqi reconstruction] work until after the 30 June transfer
of sovereignty, in part to maintain leverage over the next
Iraqi government'.[55]

Restricting Iraqi sovereignty is only one task Washington

faces after an 'independent Iraq' is established. Another 'major challenge is sorting out the terms of the US military presence, which is expected to exceed 100,000 troops even after the occupation ends, US officials say'. Without reading the US press, Iraqis can also understand that US officials 'do not expect the transfer of political power to lead to a short-term reduction in US military might there' and that the United States has 'rejected the notion that handing over political power is the first step toward an immediate withdrawal of forces, citing ongoing security needs'.[56]

The last phrase is for the US audience. To lend it credibility, some facts have to be avoided: crucially, that Iraqis want Iraqis to take responsibility for 'security needs', so we learn from one of the most extensive Western-run polls.[57] It was reported, but keeping to useful trivialities (e.g., that people are happy to be rid of the tyrant, which we know without polls). The poll also found that although 'people overwhelmingly worry about their security and the spectre of drifting into chaos . . . less than 1% worry about occupation forces actually leaving' and 60 percent want Iraqis to be in charge of security (7 percent prefer US forces, 5 percent other 'coalition' forces, and 5 percent the US-appointed Governing Council). In general, 'People have no confidence in US/UK forces (79%) and the Coalition Provisional Authority – CPA (73%). 8% say they have a "great deal" of faith in US/UK troops. They also mistrust Iraqi political parties (78%). While still largely mistrusted, the UN scores relatively best among non-Iraqi institutions (35% confidence).' Pentagon favorite Ahmed Chalabi had no detectable support; in contrast, 'Saddam Hussein remains one of the six most popular politicians in the country.' In another poll, 57 percent said they would support 'Arab forces' providing security.[58]

When asked what Iraq needs right now, over 70 percent 'strongly agree' with the choice 'democracy', while 10 percent choose the CPA and 15 percent the Governing Council.[59] And by 'democracy' they mean democracy, not the façade of nominal sovereignty that the 'Idealist in Chief' and his colleagues are designing.

The US–Iraqi conflict over sovereignty was highly visible at the first anniversary of the invasion. Wolfowitz and his Pentagon staff 'are signalling that they favor a sizable, prolonged US troop presence there and a relatively weak Iraqi army as the best way to nurture democracy', where the phrase 'nurture democracy' is to be understood in the style of Wolfowitz's reprimand to the Turkish military: its beneficiaries have to 'salute and shout, "Yes sir" . . . We have to please America no matter what the cost', as explained by a high Latvian official when asked why Latvia agreed to send troops to Iraq over enormous public opposition. Even the US-appointed 'interim leaders', bowing to public demands, say 'they could not negotiate a formal agreement with the American military on maintaining troops in Iraq', a task that must be left to a 'sovereign Iraqi government'. That poses a serious problem for Wolfowitz-style democracy: 'The delay could put the Americans in the position of negotiating an agreement with leaders they did not appoint on such sensitive issues as when the use of force would be allowed.'[60]

From the outset, the United States had been 'planning a long-term military relationship with the emerging government of Iraq, one that would grant the Pentagon access to military bases and project American influence into the heart of the unsettled region, senior Bush administration officials say'. The plans have faced firm resistance from Iraqis, part of their steadfast effort to gain more than the nominal sovereignty that the United States has in mind for them. This resistance, rather than bombs and killings, may have been the most serious problem facing Washington, a fact occasionally recognized.[61]

There would have been no point in the invasion in the first place if it did not lead to an 'Arab façade' with 'top-down democracy' run by elite elements linked to the United States, with stable US military bases. Washington is particularly concerned about Iraqi demands that 'directly elected representatives' approve any military agreement that would 'allow more than 100,000 American troops to remain in the country after power is handed over to the Iraqis' in July 2004. Washington planners hoped, somehow, to tweak the 'caucus system [effectively under US control] to look more democratic without changing it in a fundamental way'. The UN may be brought in, but Washington is asking it 'to endorse a future Iraqi government of only nominal sovereignty and questionable legitimacy, by whose invitation the occupying powers would remain in place'.[62] 'Nurturing democracy' in that style is never an easy sell.

US officials, at last report, 'say they believe they have found a legal basis for American troops to continue their military control over the security situation in Iraq'; to translate to simple English, to maintain their military presence despite strong Iraqi popular opposition, so as to control the region and keep a firm hand on the 'stupendous source of strategic power' that it offers for world control. Bremer ordered that Iraqi forces be placed under US command, claiming frivolous Security Council authorization.[63]

While watching US efforts to maintain control through diplomatic and military means, Iraqis can also see the modalities imposed to eliminate economic sovereignty, including a series of orders from Bremer to open up industries and banks to effective US takeover, and impose a flat tax of 15 percent. This 'stunning [plan] would immediately make Iraq's economy one of the most open to trade and capital flows in the world, and put it among the lowest taxed in the world, rich or poor', virtually eliminating the hope for funding of desperately needed social benefits and infrastructure, economist Jeff Madrick writes. The plan is 'supported neither by theory nor experience, only by the wishful ideological thinking of its advocates', with consequences that 'could be widespread cruelty'. Not surprisingly, the plans 'were immediately attacked by Iraqi business representatives', who charged that they would 'destroy the role of the Iraqi industrialist'.[64]

There may be fewer problems with Iraqi workers. The occupying army quickly took action to destroy the unions, breaking into offices and arresting leaders, blocking strikes, enforcing Saddam's brutal anti-labor laws, handing over concessions to bitterly anti-union US businesses, and in general ensuring that there will be no interference with approved economic policies from the underlying population.[65] Nevertheless, strong Iraqi resistance and the remarkable failures of the military occupation caused Washington to backtrack somewhat from the more extreme proposals.[66]

The proposals to open up the economy to effective foreign takeover excluded oil. Presumably that would have been too brazen. However, Iraqis do not have to read the Western business press to discover that 'getting to know Iraq's ravaged oil industry in detail', thanks to lucrative

Noam Chomsky

contracts provided them by US taxpayers, 'eventually could help Halliburton win mainstream energy business there', along with other state-supported MNCs.[67]

It remains to be seen whether Iraqis can be coerced into accepting the 'nominal sovereignty' that is offered them under the various 'constitutional fictions' that are devised by the occupying power. Another question is far more important for privileged Westerners: will they permit their governments to 'nurture democracy' in the interests of the narrow sectors of power they serve, over strong Iraqi opposition? Will the large majority of Americans who support the decision of the Spanish voters in March 2004 find a way to enter their own political system? These matters extend far beyond Iraq: to terror and intervention elsewhere, to weapons development, and to a host of other policies that threaten decent survival. And to domestic affairs as well. It is no secret that a major domestic problem is the exploding health care costs in the mostly privatized US system, far higher than comparable societies and with relatively poor outcomes, results traceable in large measure to the enormous inefficiencies of privatization and the control of the government by the pharmaceutical industry, which tops the profit ranking year after year. As in the past, large majorities favor national health insurance, most regarding it as a 'moral issue'. Eighty percent regard universal health care as 'more important than holding down taxes', and favor legal imports of prescription drugs. But if these questions arise at all, the proposals are held to be 'politically impossible', because of 'tangled politics'. That is true: disentangling the politics, we discover that the pharmaceutical industry, insurance companies, and other private powers will not allow it, so the will of the public is out of the political arena.[68]

Realities, 2004

These are among the many signs of serious erosion of a democratic culture under dedicated multi-pronged assaults. Americans are hardly less able to confront such problems than landless workers in Brazil, Haitian peasants, and many others: today Iraqis. There is no need to linger on what is at stake as they confront the severe and growing democratic deficit in the world's most powerful state.

Noam Chomsky
April 2004

For the notes to accompany
Doctrines and Visions please go to
www.happybirthdaypenguin.com

POCKET PENGUINS

1. Lady Chatterley's Trial
2. **Eric Schlosser** Cogs in the Great Machine
3. **Nick Hornby** Otherwise Pandemonium
4. **Albert Camus** Summer in Algiers
5. **P. D. James** Innocent House
6. **Richard Dawkins** The View from Mount Improbable
7. **India Knight** On Shopping
8. **Marian Keyes** Nothing Bad Ever Happens in Tiffany's
9. **Jorge Luis Borges** The Mirror of Ink
10. **Roald Dahl** A Taste of the Unexpected
11. **Jonathan Safran Foer** The Unabridged Pocketbook of Lightning
12. **Homer** The Cave of the Cyclops
13. **Paul Theroux** Two Stars
14. **Elizabeth David** Of Pageants and Picnics
15. **Anaïs Nin** Artists and Models
16. **Antony Beevor** Christmas at Stalingrad
17. **Gustave Flaubert** The Desert and the Dancing Girls
18. **Anne Frank** The Secret Annexe
19. **James Kelman** Where I Was
20. **Hari Kunzru** Noise
21. **Simon Schama** The Bastille Falls
22. **William Trevor** The Dressmaker's Child
23. **George Orwell** In Defence of English Cooking
24. **Michael Moore** Idiot Nation
25. **Helen Dunmore** Rose, 1944
26. **J. K. Galbraith** The Economics of Innocent Fraud
27. **Gervase Phinn** The School Inspector Calls
28. **W. G. Sebald** Young Austerlitz
29. **Redmond O'Hanlon** Borneo and the Poet
30. **Ali Smith** Ali Smith's Supersonic 70s
31. **Sigmund Freud** Forgetting Things
32. **Simon Armitage** King Arthur in the East Riding
33. **Hunter S. Thompson** Happy Birthday, Jack Nicholson
34. **Vladimir Nabokov** Cloud, Castle, Lake
35. **Niall Ferguson** 1914: Why the World Went to War

POCKET PENGUINS